BEING DIFFERENT IS FUN

By Celia Kibler

Illustrations by Aquil Khan

©2020 Celia Kibler

Published Proudly in the United States of America
Copyright ©Celia Kibler 2020
All rights reserved.

This book cannot be copied, resold or redistributed without prior consent of its author.

This book is dedicated:

To all the humans that roam this earth,
That come out different from their birth.
Here's to your uniqueness, here's to your fame,
And here's to everything else, that makes us the same.

Each person is different,
from their front to their back.
There are all kinds of colors,
from white through to black.

Some are tall as a tree,

some are short as a fern,

but we're all quite the same,

when we take time to learn.

Our hair might be wavy,

or curly or flat,

or no hair at all,

some wear a cool hat.

Our lips might be tiny,

or puffy or big.

Our nose might be large,

or thin as a twig.

Our arms might be short,

or really quite long.

Our legs might be weak,

or really quite strong.

Our teeth might be crooked,

or straight as an arrow.

Our ears might stick out,

or look kind of narrow.

We all can communicate,

in one way or another,

a tickle from Dad,

or big hugs from our Mother.

The language we speak,

is taught when we're small.

And some use their hands,

'cause they don't speak at all.

Whether you're black,

white, yellow or blue,

it's the way that you act,

when you meet someone new.

It's important to listen,

and learn what they're like,

'cause you may just find out,

you're so much alike.

Inside of us all,
are two really big things,
that keep us alive,
and gives us our wings.

It's a superpower we have,
so we all do our part,
to understand and love,
through our brains and our heart.

Now be sure when you're talking,
to someone you've met,
who may seem a bit different,
'cause you don't know them yet.

Offer them a smile,
and find out their name.
And talk to each other,
to see what's the same.

We all have our genius,

our visions and dreams,

and there's always hope,

no matter how hopeless it seems.

Reach out to your neighbor,

they're your sister and brother.

The only difference is,

they're not from your mother.

So go and ride bikes,

play cards, tag or run,

'cause when you get down to it,

being different is fun!

About the Author

Celia Kibler is the Author of RAISING HAPPY TODDLERS: How to Gain Great Parenting Skills and Stop Yelling at Your Kids. Her children's books include Being Different is Fun, All About Me and I Am Grateful. She is the Founder of Pumped Up Parenting (2016) and Funfit® Family Fitness (1987).

Celia is the Mom of 5 kids; 2 she gave birth to & 3 she gained from marriage; as well as a Grandma of 9. She has successfully parented a blended family for over 24 years.

As a Family Empowerment Coach, Celia is on a Mission to stop 1,000,000 parents from yelling at their kids and specializes in creating cooperative childhoods that everyone in the family can blossom from.

As a child, Celia wore a body brace for 5 years for Scoliosis (immediately following wearing a neck brace for her teeth for 3 years) and experienced first-hand how being different can either make you miserable or empower you to be more. It was during this time that she gained the outlook on life of gratitude and always being one to see the glass as half full, not half empty. Her childhood was full of diversity, always welcoming foreign exchange students into her home for years at a time and being consistently introduced to a variety of cultures, learning first-hand how being different is so much fun.

With over 40 years of coaching, teaching, counseling kids and their parents including Special Needs populations, Celia's love for children is evident in every aspect of her life.

She truly loves to rhyme (to the point that it drives her own kids a little crazy), but this gift and her understanding of how children's minds work, has led her to write many children's books, with more on the way.

Connect with Celia on all Social Media outlets... YT, FB, IG, LI, Pinterest
celia@celiakibler.com
www.CeliaKibler.com
www.PumpedUpParentiting.com
www.Funfifit.com

More books by Celia Kibler available on Amazon

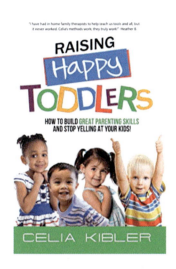
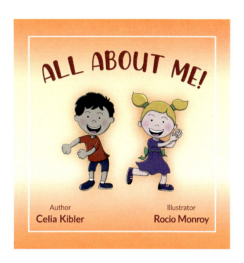
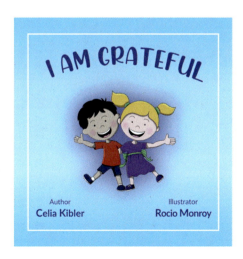

Made in the USA
Columbia, SC
14 February 2022